A u

B

MW00595366

*Cherish the
memories.*

Bette

A Memoir

Writers
At Last

Lillian Lindy
Nancy Mather
Bette Marafino
Ketti Marks

*"Preserve your memories, keep them well,
what you forget you can never retell."*

Louisa May Alcott

Our Book

The university where we met offers lots of classes for those of a certain age. In the fall of 2016 two of us decided to register for Memoir Writing because we wanted to "whip" our childhood stories into shape. For six weeks we wrote – for sharing, for learning, and sometimes for catharsis. We are still writing, and two others have joined us on this journey of personal exploration. So here we are—Catholic and Jewish, believers and nonbelievers, with roots in America and roots in Europe, each of us with sixty plus years of memories. As we write these "memos," as one of our husbands calls them, we smile or shed tears, fueled by all that is sentient. We have become great friends, sharing.

Each of us wondered if it was too late to embark on this project. We did a little research and discovered that some of the books we had read as children such as *Black Beauty* by Anna Sewell and *Little House on the Prairie* by Laura Ingalls Wilder were written well into their authors' prime.

We believe there is no age limit on creativity or expressions of the human heart, and we take joy in knowing that today, in the year 2020, words still matter. And so we write about the moments in our lives, ordinary and extraordinary, that have brought us to where we are today. We begin in the World War II years and continue into the present day. Each of our stories was inspired by a memory that sparked our emotions and made us want to cry or laugh or do it all over again.

Acknowledgments

It's been quite a ride on the Memory Wheel. Our thanks go to Lora Lee for her expertise in graphic design and layout, and to Beth Richards, whose memoir class at the University of Hartford's Presidents' College is where it all began. Once we embarked on the project, Harrison Library Director Randi Aston-Pritting provided us with much-needed space to work and encouragement.

Special thanks to the Australian War Memorial, the United States National Archives, and the Project Gutenberg library for compiling the compelling historical and literary images that helped us tell our stories. Shutterstock's large collection of photos, vectors, and illustrations was an invaluable source of visuals.

We are especially indebted to Albert Einstein, Oscar Wilde, and Stephen King for their profound reflections on the human condition. Finally, we cannot forget William Shakespeare's fun-loving Puck, whose words so beautifully captured that moment of self-recognition when we walked out of one world and into another.

We will always be grateful to our friends and family for their unending love and support as we put pen to paper to reconnect with the past.

Writers At Last

Copyright © 2020 Lillian Lindy, Nancy Mather,
Bette Marafino, and Ketti Marks

All rights reserved. This book or any portion thereof
may not be reproduced or used in any manner whatsoever
without the express written permission of the publisher
except for the use of brief quotations in a book review.

Book Design by Lora Lee

Printed in the United States of America

First Printing, 2020

ISBN 978-0-9907376-2-9 (paperback)

Published by 4WUH

Contents

"I know not with what weapons World War III will be fought, but World War IV will be fought with sticks and stones."

Albert Einstein

CHAPTER 1

War Effects

War is a confounding experience for children. This was as true seventy-five years ago as it is today. Children know deep inside when something is wrong. Some ask questions while others become silent although their inner selves may be roiling.

What follows are our memories of those difficult years when the Second World War impacted everyone, even the very young. We write, too, of those years when our invasion of Vietnam led to protests that shook the nation. Today, all of us share poet Eve Merriam's dream of a planet where a child will ask, "Mother, what was war?"

Trauma

Lillian Lindy

I was three and a half years old when World War II broke out. Did I even know what was happening? Surely not, because at that age war is not comprehensible. The little I do remember are the air raids, the dive bombings of planes, the sounds of destruction. We were living in Paris and when there was an air raid, we and the other twelve families in our building descended to the dark basement. My father carried me down, and I remember the fear that gripped me as I clung to his neck. I hated being in the dark and hearing the noise overhead, but I am sure that being with my family consoled me a little. Even so, these bombings had a lasting effect. I was scared of thunder well into my 60s.

In 1940, we went to the South of France as so many people did to get away from the Nazi occupation of Paris. I don't recall any fear while being there. The South was Vichy controlled, but not German occupied. We left Nice by car en route to Portugal. One night, in fascist Spain, we slept in a gypsy cave and I remember my mother telling us not to eat or drink anything because she feared it was poisoned. All I remember is that it was dark and creepy.

In Portugal, we boarded the *US Excalibur*. It left late at night. Our parents told us that the boat would not leave unless we were sleeping. Years later I learned that departing at night was the best way to get into the Atlantic and away from where the German U-boats were. The Atlantic Ocean

Leaving Europe Behind

List of Passengers Cover, SS Excalibur
I traveled on the SS Excalibur on July 18, 1941.

On May 1, 1942 the ship was acquired by the U.S. Navy
and used as a troop transport. It was sunk by the Germans
in a torpedo attack on November 11, 1942.

War Damage Report #32 Naval History and Heritage Command

was a deadly area for ships during the war.

I was only five when we arrived in the United States. I recall some sort of food rationing but most of all I remember saving aluminum foil and rubber bands for the war effort. I was nine when the war ended. My parents never discussed the war, probably because they wanted to protect me.

It was really not until I was a young teenager that I began to understand what had happened. In the early 1950s I lived in France for two years, and met many people who had survived the war; some had lost family and friends due to the Nazi horrors. Ever since then I have had a big interest in the cataclysmic events of World War II. I have read many books about the Holocaust, and have visited the D Day beaches in Normandy, and the American Cemetery. My life in many ways was defined by this war, as was my husband's, who was in Pearl Harbor when it was attacked by the Japanese. Visiting Pearl Harbor, my husband broke down and sobbed recalling his terrible experience.

Many years after these visits, I began looking into my past, and learned that my grandfather and his brother were both burned at Auschwitz.

A Photographic Studio in Brooklyn

Nancy Mather

In May of 1941 I was 11 years old. My father had emigrated from Italy to the United States in 1921 at the age of 17. In America, he worked as a stone carver, carving letters and embellishments on granite and marble headstones. In the '30s, though, it was becoming evident that stone carvers were prone to lung disease. By that time, he had a family to support and he was not willing to jeopardize his health. He had always been interested in photography, and he enrolled in the New School in New York City to learn the art of portrait photography. In November of 1941 he opened a portrait studio in Brooklyn, where we lived.

Barely a month later on December 7, 1941, the Japanese attacked Pearl Harbor and the United States began conscripting young men over the age of 18 in order to build its army. Women joined the Army, Navy, and Air Force and became WACS, WAVES, and WASPS. Other women worked in the factories replacing the men who had gone off to war. Rosie the Riveter stood as the symbol of those women.

Although we did not have family members in the thick of war, our family did experience the pain of loss over and over again when a mother, wife, or other family member visited the studio to tell my father about the death, wounding, or missing in action status of a beautiful young man he had photographed. Taking portraits of these young men were intimate moments for him and so he was deeply saddened

Where I Saw War

A NYC Landmark

upon learning of their loss or wounding. I had also come to know many of them as they waited to be photographed.

Since help was scarce, my younger sister and I often helped out in the studio. In the darkroom we rinsed freshly printed photographs to remove the chemical residue. After school and on weekends I took incoming calls at the desk, made appointments, and welcomed customers. I also took the subway to Manhattan where I would go to Medo and Willoughbys, the photographic supply stores, to buy the paper and chemicals my father needed for his work. These could not be purchased in bulk during the war.

In 1948, at the age of 18, I met Steve, who had earned a Purple Heart and Bronze Star as a result of his service during the war. We married in April 1951. We had three children and a happy marriage for nineteen years. He died in May 1970.

Sometimes I wonder if the time I spent in my father's studio during the war, a time when I saw so much grief, made me better able to handle the loss of my husband years later. I had been young, but I had learned an important lesson: life is intangible, pick up and keep on going.

War in the Womb

Bette Marafino

As long as I've been alive, war of one sort or another has been omnipresent. World War II, Korea, Vietnam, Iraq, Afghanistan and our involvement in Kosovo have been constants. Sometimes it seems that one war ends and the other begins.

One of my earliest memories was when I was five and a half and learning from my parents about this big war in a faraway place called Europe. My mother's older brother Lefty was in the U.S. Army, stationed somewhere in Europe and as we later learned, had fought in the Battle of the Bulge.

Why do I remember this so vividly? In late 1943 and the spring of 1944, my mother was expecting her third child. Mom, being a nervous person, was especially nervous and anxious during this pregnancy, not because anything was physically wrong, but because she was worried about Uncle Lefty. Lefty was his nickname; his given name was Vincent.

Because communication between soldiers and folks back home was erratic, weeks would go by without any communication. Mom knew bad news came by telegram or a knock on the door accompanied by a soldier in uniform as the bearer of bad news.

"I don't like listening to the news; it makes me so nervous."

That was my mother's usual comment about the war. Mom said this often, and I remember her being startled whenever the doorbell rang. We lived on the third floor of an apartment

Uncle Lefty in Europe

Stressed From the Start

house and when the doorbell rang, we couldn't see who was at the door until we went downstairs. Believe me, those were anxious trips.

My sister Bernadette was born on D-Day, June 6, 1944, and came out screaming, and that's what she did every day for the next six months.

"Wheel your sister around, so I can make dinner."

This was often the greeting when I came home from first grade that fall. My poor mother was so worn out from my sister's crying that she desperately needed a break. My four-year old sister Mary and I took turns wheeling the carriage through the kitchen, into the dining room, through the hallway, past the bedrooms and back into the kitchen. Round and round we pushed until our sister was quiet. All this is to suggest that I believe learning takes place in the womb, and that my mother's agitated state during pregnancy left its imprint on my baby sister.

I remember going to a parade in New Britain with my parents, sister Mary, and Bernadette, who was nestled in her carriage. We stood on the steps of St. Mary's Church, a good viewing spot because that's where the marching units came around the corner, marched down the incline, passed the church and usually struck up a tune. On this occasion, one of the marching units fired off a few rounds. Pow! Boom!! collided with the horns and drums of the marching band. This set my sister off; she became a kicking, shrieking baby and her cries almost drowned out the band. My father took off with her in the carriage attempting to get her as far away from the noise as possible. For many years after, Bernadette was startled by loud noises. Were these sounds reminiscent of the war that had so plagued my mother? All the doctors who treated my sister in her infancy could not find any physical cause for her crying and reaction to loud noises.

Uncle Lefty returned home safely when the war ended, and until his death a few years ago, never wanted to talk about his war experiences. A few years ago I visited the World War II Memorial in Washington, D.C.

This impressive monument, which honors those in the European and Pacific theaters has 4,048 gold stars that remind us of the price these Americans paid to win that war. World War I was supposed to be the war to end all wars; sadly that did not prove to be true. 🌷

Coming of Age During Vietnam

Ketti Marks

I grew up in the years following World War II. My discomfort with the norm began when I saw a fish-pale man in shirt sleeves yelling on television. It was Joseph McCarthy. I was only five or six years old, but his image repelled me. In school a few years later, I never quite bought the lesson that America was all good and Russia was all bad, which probably explains why a boy in my fourth-grade class liked to trip me and then mutter "dirty Communist" under his breath. At 12, I discovered I had been nixed by the Brownies at my old elementary school because the PTA was convinced that my mother was too liberal to be anything but a Communist. Six years later, after the Vietnam War had come into our living rooms, I heard that word a lot.

When I was 18, the Student Peace Union, or SPU as we called it, became the center of my universe. It all began at the behest of my sister who at the same age had done her bit for liberal movements, including a stint at YPSL, the Young People's Socialist League, where she had met people like Michael Harrington and Bayard Rustin. So I wasn't surprised that winter day when she decided it was time for some sisterly advice.

I was curled up in my favorite blue chair doing a crossword puzzle when she asked,

"Can't you find something better to do when you come home from school?"

It became a topic of conversation at dinner, "What should Ketti do with her spare time?"

This soon evolved into a discussion of the domino theory and democracy and what the hell were we doing in Vietnam anyway? Over spaghetti one night I told my parents I had made my decision: I was going to join the anti-war movement. They thought that was a great idea, especially my father who had gotten arrested a few times during the Depression for sitting in at relief bureaus. And that's how I ended up at the Student Peace Union, located at 5 Beekman Street, just a few blocks west of the Manhattan side of the Brooklyn Bridge.

It was an exciting time for me at 5 Beekman. That first day at SPU I met Rob from Massachusetts. Then I met Marc, a young man with razor-sharp blue eyes who had made the front page of the New York Times for burning his draft card.

Rob said, "Hi, welcome to our home away from home."

Marc eyed me for a moment and said, "Ditto."

After Marc left, Rob began to explain things. He pointed across the hall to Tom Cornell's office.

"Tom is managing editor of the *Catholic Worker*. He organized the first demonstration against the war. Let's go for a walk and I'll show you some more."

Soon, we stopped to say hello to Ralph DiGia, a conscientious objector who had spent time in a federal prison during World War II. I liked Ralph right away. He was a sweet-looking man with gray hair and an easy smile. He asked me a few questions about school. Then he wanted to know how I had found my way to SPU. I told him that my family could take credit for that.

When Rob and I continued down the hall, we stopped

And so We Asked, Where Have All the Flowers Gone?

Where Have All The Flowers Gone is the title of a folk song written by Pete Seeger. It was sung by anti-Vietnam protesters at marches and rallies. Other anti-Vietnam songs include *Blowing in the Wind*, and *Give Peace A Chance.*

Images courtesy of Dr. Richard Ostreicher,
Professor Emeritus, University of Pittsburgh.

in front of A.J. Muste's office. I stood stock still. I knew the
name. I respected the man whose name it was. I said to
myself, This is it. I am in the movement.

Time passed, and I rarely saw A.J. Muste. Labor activist,
Civil rights activist, Pacifist. Eighty-one years old. Perhaps he
was working hard behind that door; perhaps he only came
in a few days a week. Once, though, I saw him standing at
the mirror that hung outside his office. He had an oddly
sweet expression on his face. I watched, mesmerized, as he
slowly straightened his tie. It was just a few months later that
I attended his memorial service: the gentle titan of social
justice was gone.

Watching A.J. Muste before the mirror is a memory that has
stayed with me all these years. Some of my other memories
of that time are just as sharp but not as pleasant. I didn't
exactly fit in at SPU. I usually wore skirts and heels, the idea
of living on chicken necks in the East Village disgusted me,
and, I always said, "No thanks," when the weed was passed
around at parties. A few of the other teenagers teased me
about my conformist ways. In my mind, though, they were
the ones following the crowd, not me. But the little jabs made
me tense.

One day a few months after I started at SPU, Rob said,
"Hey, Ketti, have a cigarette."

I took a puff. On the second puff, I inhaled. I didn't like
the menthol. So the next day I bought my own pack of
cigarettes – just tar and nicotine, no menthol. I don't think
Rob was trying to get me hooked. But that's what happened.
My mistake, not his.

Another time, I was sitting against the wall in my stockings and purple dress with the white sailor collar, minding my own business and stuffing envelopes, when Marc passed by.

"You'll get goosed sitting there like that," he said with a smile.

I didn't know what he meant. Or what he had in mind, but I soon learned. It started with a light touch on the Staten Island Ferry. Then there was a trip to his family's house in Westchester where I met his mother. Finally, we visited his friend Peter. And Peter's loft bed. After a while, Marc moved on to his next victim. But what appalled me more than anything about Marc was what happened one fall afternoon when I went to the office to drop off some leaflets. Marc was there alone. He told me there had been a fire there the night before.

"Was anyone hurt?" I asked.

"No," he said, "Marsha took the files and ran."

"She should have just run."

Marc looked at me disdainfully and said,

"Those files are more important than her life."

I almost left the movement after that encounter. But I stayed because at this small building not far from the Brooklyn Bridge, I had met people whose politics were akin to my own. For the first time, I felt free to say what I wanted about things that would earn me a caustic remark or a frown somewhere else. I could talk about civil rights or Emma Goldman or the fact that my great aunt Minn had been the librarian at the Little Red Schoolhouse and had known the Rosenberg children who had been students there during the height of the Red Scare. I stayed because I could talk to people like Bernie and Pauline Goodman, a middle-aged couple who reminded me of my parents and made me wonder what their life-and mine- would have been like if they had decided to devote themselves to causes once youth had passed them by.

I stayed because SPU was my comfort zone. Outside, I felt more vulnerable – at lunch, when I walked the few blocks to Chinatown for my sixty-five cent bowl of Wonton Soup, in the evening, when I took the train home to Brooklyn, at the skating rink, when a guard looked at the button on my jacket and said to me bitterly,

"My brother died in Vietnam."

But it was at the rallies and demonstrations that my two worlds collided the most and left me spinning. In one, a policeman smiled kindly when he gave me directions to the subway; in the other, I watched in horror as perhaps the same policeman clubbed a middle-aged demonstrator. And on Sundays, when we handed out anti-war leaflets at the Port Authority, the same people who probably would have smiled at me on the bus, suddenly felt empowered to scream invectives.

"Go back to Russia," they would shout.

"You're all a bunch of Reds!"

Those evenings became my tutorial on mini-mob psychology.

The vitriol upset me, but it didn't stop me. It only made me want to do more. I kept protesting. My father drove me to Battery Park for a 6:00 a.m. demonstration. I went to Washington to march against the war and drank sour wine on the bus on the way back. I went to a sleep-in at Brooklyn College. The next day my picture was on page 4 of the *Post*.

I learned a lot about people in my protest days. At one

Saying No to War

rally we were all holding flowers and waiting for the light to change when a woman in a passing limousine smiled and waved at us. I couldn't believe it. Did she really think the flowers were for her? At an all-night vigil near the U.N. a man dropped his hotel keys on the ground in front of me with a knowing wink and pointed his head toward the hotel just up the street.

What alien world was he living in?

At my last demonstration, it was evening. The streets were narrow, the stores were locked, and the police were brutal. I felt as if I was struggling against a sea of angry, clubbing blue monsters. I panicked and froze, shaking. My boyfriend scooped me up and we ran by what seemed like hordes of people trying to jump into showcase windows. He turned, finally, into the quiet side street where we had parked.

At the car he said, "It'll be okay. Stay here. I'm locking the door."

As I sat there, waiting, I looked out the window. I saw a man running, and a policeman following, club raised. The man turned into the bushes. So did his pursuer. I closed my eyes. I felt sick. I knew that, for me, it was time to go home.

Six months later, I returned to college. It was years later, when I was working toward my M.A. that I met up again with Bernie and Pauline Goodman. They invited me to their apartment in Gramercy, and when I stepped into the once familiar living room, I felt as if I had been catapulted back in time. There was the armchair where Bernie had sat, plate in hand, during our potluck Sunday suppers. There was Pauline's chair, just opposite. The piano was still by the back wall, just as I had remembered.

In my final memory of that afternoon in Gramercy, Bernie, Pauline, and I are having coffee in the kitchen. It is a sunny day, and a fly is buzzing over the stove. I watch as Bernie gently ushers the fly out of the open window. I smile to myself. I had known he wouldn't kill it.

"Be yourself. Everyone else is already taken."

Oscar Wilde

CHAPTER 2

Snippets From School

All these years later, we sip our coffee and tea and reminisce about what school was like when we were young. Dick and Jane. Dress codes. Lots of rote learning. Teachers and principals who imposed strict rules. It was a system in which individuality and imagination took second place to compliance and conformity. Students were expected to obey the rules and not provoke their teachers. In elementary school we lived up to these expectations with one caveat: it was okay to make fun of a teacher if he or she wasn't looking. In high school we occasionally flouted the rules or vented. Sometimes, we even stood up and rebelled.

Memorable Moments

Lillian Lindy

Kindergarten. All I remember is that we wore uniforms and I got hit in the eye with a lunchbox.

I went to the Ethical Culture School in Manhattan from grades two through eight. No more collisions with lunchboxes. But there was Mr. Wohl. My classmates and I thoroughly disliked him, so we sang "Whistle while you work. Hitler is a Jerk, Mussolini is a Beanie, but Mr. Wohl is worse." In home economics class, I learned the basics, but when we were told to show what we had made, I panicked. I had tried to make a plaid skirt and had followed the pattern and cut very carefully, but when I went to assemble the skirt, none of the plaid pieces matched. What a disaster!! Then there was lining up. I was tall so I was the last one on line. If they had lined us up by weight, I would still be last on line, as I was a tall chunky kid when I was 11 and 12.

At Fieldston School in Riverdale, I took Spanish with Dr. Elias, a German, and we all learned to speak Spanish with a slight German accent. In biology class, we dissected all kinds of things, like a frog, a fish, even a cow's eye. I hated dissecting, but fortunately I had a partner who loved to do it. The day after I submitted my drawing of the anatomy of a frog, my paper came back with a note from the teacher who wrote, "Interesting frog – both male and female."

In my junior year, I left Fieldston to move to France. Since I was not fluent in French, I went to The American School

An Eclectic Education

American School of Paris, Founded 1946

of Paris. I had some fabulous teachers who really whetted my appetite for learning. My grades were so good that I did not have to take any final exams. What a change from a C student at Fieldston!

I came back to the United States after being away almost two years. It was time for college. At Russell Sage I was assigned to the French House because of my fluency in French. We had to speak French at all times, except when in our rooms. I am not sure everyone was interested in learning French since the first question I was asked when I arrived at the dorm was "Do you play bridge?" I didn't.

Soon I became friends with two sophomores, Barbara and Ellie, neither of whom played bridge. We were a deadly trio. What escapades we had! One of our favorites was sneaking down to the kitchen late at night and raiding the refrigerator. One night we found the refrigerator locked, so we took the door off by the hinges. Then we discovered that all access to the kitchen had been blocked. There was, however, a dumbwaiter, and Ellie, who was the smallest of the trio, would get into the dumbwaiter, and we would lower her down to the kitchen where she would open the door from the inside, and we were at it again. One time however, Ellie got into the dumbwaiter and it started to crash. Luckily, both Barbara and I had the presence of mind to grab the center rope. That was the last time we raided the kitchen. We never got caught.

I left college after my freshman year and made the first big mistake of my life by getting married – but that is another story. 🌷

It Started With a Song

Nancy Mather

I began school in September of 1936 when I was six. On the first day, my mother and I walked to our Lady of Guadalupe Grammar School, which went from first to eighth grade, and was taught by Dominican nuns.

Upon arriving at the school we made our way to the classroom where my teacher Sister Rose Monica was wearing the strangest clothes I had ever seen on anyone. She wore a long cream-colored dress with a panel of the same color. A wimple made of starched linen covered her hair, the sides of her face, and her neck. A long black veil, stiffened by a linen lining, encircled and framed her head. There was a round white collar circling her neck, and a long black rosary hung from a belt around her waist. I don't remember being put off by this oddly dressed woman for she had a warm, welcoming smile and greeted me by name.

I can still picture my first grade classroom with its small wooden desks, thin colored counting pencils, and piles of copy books and readers. But most of all, I remember performing in a Christmas pageant which included a scene inspired by a Shirley Temple movie. I have many happy memories of that time, and if I close my eyes I can see Sister Rose Monica handing me a large white lollipop with a hard, red candy center which we first-graders held up high as we sang *On The Good Ship Lollipop.*

In the third grade I was accepted into the children's

A Wonderful Bygone Day Singing at Christmastime
Ms. McLaughlin (middle in dark dress) leading the choir.

church choir. I was so excited! Now I would be singing every Sunday. The choir was led by Christine McLaughlin, the church organist and an outstanding music director. She was a tall, lean woman in her mid-twenties with a beautiful voice who lived at home with her two unmarried sisters. Her sister Monica, whom I came to love, was a great influence on me. She sang with the choir and today, when I hear the Christmas carol *O Holy Night,* her voice reverberates in my head.

Under Miss McLaughlin's tutelage, our choir became well known throughout the Diocese of Brooklyn for its sound, which means many voices coming through as one voice. At Mass and on church Holy Days we sang the music of the world's renowned composers in Latin, and the Gregorian chant that I still love today. We put on shows in the school auditorium where we sang the popular songs from the Broadway musicals of the day. We made recordings and sang on radio.

Singing with the choir from third grade into young adulthood gave me an understanding and love for classical music. It was a happy time and I believe may have spared me the usual adolescent angst. It was in my early teens, due to the influence of my father, that I became the opera lover that I am today. In season I would take the subway early on a Saturday morning to go to the Metropolitan Opera House and wait in line for that afternoon's standing room tickets. Once the curtain rose and the opera began, I would position myself behind the orchestra seats because at times people would leave midway through the performance.

Many years later I was with my children at a Sunday Mass at La Madeleine in Paris when I heard the choir sing music

I'll Always Remember Ms. McLaughlin

that brought back the memory of a Latin Mass I had sung as a child. I was transfixed.

I stayed in the choir throughout high school, and for a few years after that. When I married, the choir sang at my wedding. I have never forgotten those years when I sang my heart out in church. Because sometimes, just like that morning in Paris, a song jolts my memory, and I feel like a young girl again, made rapt by music. 🌱

2.74

Bette Marafino

It's not the unfortunate incident with my underpants in kindergarten, nor my music teacher asking me to "pretend" at my 4th grade strings concert. Instead I want to write about the private academic embarrassment that haunts me to this day.

2.74 was not an unlucky lottery number. It was my final grade point average for my studies as an Education major at what was then Teacher's College of Connecticut, now Central Connecticut State University. Up to this point, I've only shared this embarrassment with my husband. We graduated together; he as a Dean's List student and me with my mediocre GPA.

Why 2.74? Could I have done better? I think so and when I see the GPAs and honor roll plaudits of my children and five college graduate grandchildren, including one Phi Beta Kappa holder, I am proud and happy they did not squander their time in school.

I was an Honor Society student at New Britain High School. I guess I thought college would be easy. My heart was set on becoming an elementary school teacher. I often said to myself, *Hurry up and get these education classes over so you can begin student teaching.*

For Dr. Bomhoff's Contemporary Issues course, our textbook was the *New York Times* where we concentrated on politics and important news events. At the time, I had little

It Took Me a While

interest in politics and the news, and I contributed nothing to class discussion, which was a big component of the final grade. In my Greek and Roman Mythology class we had tons of reading required and I found the subject matter dull and confusing. Years later when I was teaching my Introduction to Literature classes at Tunxis Community College my feelings were so different. I relished bringing these gods and goddesses into class discussions.

Living at home didn't help. My two sisters were in high school and middle school and I fell into the rhythm of their study habits. My mother usually chimed in with "Time for bed; you're tired." So ready or not, we went to bed.

None of the above are excuses for my mediocre grades. I'm to blame. Is there a lesson to be learned? Yes. No matter where you are in your educational journey, make it the focus of your attention. I'm now taking courses in the Presidents' College at the University of Hartford and have become a more interested student and appreciative of all the good opportunities out there to become a life-long learner.

The Sound of My Voice, The Scratch of My Pen

Ketti Marks

In the November I was 12, I concluded that 8th grade was my prelude to hell. I hated standing behind Miss McCarthy and staring into the dead eyes of a dead mink that should have been running around somewhere rather than gracing my teacher's neck.

Where was the rest of that mink? I pondered. Had its leftover skin and bones been tossed in the trash? Even its feet? And if Miss McCarthy had to wear fur couldn't she have found something without a face?

I decided that Miss McCarthy wasn't an animal lover. A fatal flaw in my opinion.

In March, she switched coats and collars.

Good, I thought to myself. Things were definitely looking up in Miss McCarthy's class. But then she dropped the bombshell.

"You girls," Miss McCarthy announced, "will be making your graduation dresses."

We gave a collective moan. It wasn't fair. The boys would be learning how to cut wood and position T-Squares and we would be learning how to cut fabric and position pins. By April, we hadn't accomplished much. Miss McCarthy did her best to reassure us.

"Have a little patience," she said. "You will all have beautiful graduation dresses by June."

And we did. Because after three months of fumbling

with patterns and foot pedals, and swearing at recalcitrant bobbins, Miss McCarthy must have realized she had given most of us an impossible task.

"Okay, girls," she said, "take the dresses home and work on them there."

We all breathed a great sigh of relief and took our dresses home to our mothers.

But I forgave Miss McCarthy for that sewing debacle because earlier that year she had done something wonderful. She had introduced me to the beauty of the spoken word.

I was a child who had already fallen in love with words, from my favorite fairy tale book filled with ogres and princesses to the adventures of Nancy Drew and Judy Bolton. I adored Sherlock Holmes and his friend Dr. Watson so much that one of my goals in life was to visit 221B Baker Street. Perhaps one day I would write stories like *The Speckled Band* or *The Red-Head League.*

Then in March, Miss McCarthy introduced us to Shakespeare, and I fell in love with words all over again. It happened the day she sat in her wooden teacher's chair while we whispered passages from *Julius Caesar* in her ear. When it was my turn, I bent down and softly recited Marullus' biting words to the fickle Roman crowd:

"You blocks, you stones, you worse than senseless things! O you hard hearts, you cruel men of Rome..."

And when I stopped, I was hooked on cadence, something that had begun years earlier in the 4th grade when I raised my hand and asked Miss Smith if I could read the psalm about the shepherd. Miss Smith had smiled like the proverbial Cheshire cat as she handed me the Bible. In her mind, I had

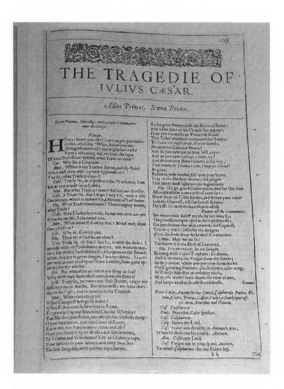

Finding My Voice

*Photo of first page of Julius Caesar from a facsimile edition of the
First Folio of Shakespeare. Original edition published in 1623, Norton
facsimile edition published 1996. Photo taken by Cowardly Lion.
CC BY-SA 2.5 PD-US-expired.*

gotten religion; it would never occur to her that I had simply fallen in love with poetry. But that is what happened. And my experience in Miss McCarthy's class was simply a more mature awareness of just how magical words can be.

There was never another Miss McCarthy. In the fall, I started high school. I was sure that I would be a star English student. I had been writing forever. I got a charge out of poetry. I didn't think there was any limit to what I could do with words, written or otherwise. On a sunny morning in mid-September my English teacher, Mr. Rosa, returned our first assignment.

I thought to myself, I'll get at least a 90. I was wrong. He handed me a paper all marked up and said quietly, but with a contemptuous sneer,

"You're in Honor's English?"

I went cold inside. Three and a half years later, at January graduation, I was awarded a certificate for excellence in English. I felt happy. I felt vindicated. Not only because I had been so devastated by Mr. Rosa's scathing question but because I felt as if I had just given Dr. Serota, one of my senior English teachers, a punch in the gut. Which he deserved.

Dr. Serota was an ordinary man with a red face who only smiled when he thought he was going to get you. My sister had been in his class at our high school four years earlier, and she warned me about him.

"Officially," she said, "he's an English teacher. Unofficially, he's a master of insult."

Leave it to my sister to sum him up so precisely. So in September of my senior year, I sat quietly in my seat and listened as he pontificated. He liked to stand by the window and assure us in a booming voice that we were all cats and dogs who would be climbing all over the walls if it weren't for him. Really, he said that!

Dr. Serota didn't talk much about novels or plays or poetry; he didn't have time. He was too busy trying to terrify us. One of his strategies was to make us grovel. If we whispered, he would thrust an "I Am Sorry" card on our desk, and say, "Read it aloud." Most of us did.

That October, Dr. Serota assigned our first novel, Thomas Hardy's *Return of the Native*. A few weeks later, after berating us for our limited understanding of how to write a grammatically correct sentence, he popped me out of my usual half-reverie.

"Ketti, write your vocabulary sentence for ennui on the board," he called from the front of the room.

I went to the side blackboard and wrote a sentence that went something like this: *Eustacia walked slowly on the heath, full of ennui, dragged down by her conviction that life here, in this little town, would soon become unbearable.* I started to read my sentence aloud, as we usually did, but Dr. Serota stopped me.

He said in an imperious voice, "Your sentence is too long. It's a run-on."

"No, it's not," I replied.

I began to explain but he cut me off.

"Down, girl! Down, girl!" he yelled from the front of the room.

I was furious, blind-red angry. I turned on my heel and walked back to my seat where he was waiting.

Ketti Teaching Debate
Years later, Ketti (2nd from the left) teaching students to have their say.

I looked straight at him, biting off every word, "You're the worst teacher I have ever had."

The class gasped. He glared. A nanosecond later, his face turned crimson and his mustache began quivering. We watched, fascinated, as his fury flew out of him like a bat out of hell. Then he pulled himself together and put one of his apology cards on my desk. I sat, silent. Carol, the girl at the desk behind me, whispered,

"Read it, Ketti."

I shook my head. From that day on, we were at war.

He called on me for everything. He thought he could get me, but he never did. Most of the time, I hated going to his class. I would pause briefly outside the door, and take a deep breath, steeling myself to endure forty-five minutes of misery.

Sometimes, though, I welcomed the challenge. I still remember the day he asked for a volunteer to conduct a lesson from Hardy's novel on why Eustacia leaves her husband. I was out of my seat before he could even say my name. A few weeks later he asked if anyone had seen a good movie recently. He looked at me. I looked at him. I smiled inside, and got up. I had seen *Tom Jones* on Saturday. Today was Monday. I was still drooling over Albert Finney and the sexy eating scene. I gave it my all. Dr. Serota actually complimented me on my enthusiastic review. That was a surprise. The even bigger surprise came at the end of the term when he called me up to his desk.

He said, "I'm sorry I've been so hard on you."

I think he meant it. But my sixteen-year-old self knew that it would happen again. He would never give up the pleasure he got from making his students squirm.

I despised Dr. Serota that semester, not only because he tried every which way to humiliate me but because he was as abruptly dismissive of my writing as Mr. Rosa had been my freshman year. I loved words, I loved what my pen could put to paper. I loved the emotional energy I got from writing. But because of Dr. Serota's fiendish classroom style, I took no joy in any writing I did that fall.

The energy came back, of course. Even today, I am driven when I write. That pleases me. I sometimes spend hours at the keyboard interrupted only by the phone and brief trips to the kitchen for sustenance. I think the need to write has always been with me. But it wasn't until I whispered Shakespeare in Miss McCarthy's ear that I found the actress in me.

Thank you, Miss McCarthy, mink scarf and all. Without that day when you sat near the closet and I whispered in your ear, you probably would have faded into the woodwork of my memory.

" A bird sitting on a tree is never afraid of the branch breaking, because its trust is not on the branch but on its own wings. "

Unattributed

CHAPTER 3

Free to Be Me

One of our favorite books is Charlotte Bronte's *Jane Eyre.* Now that we have lived a little, we admire the title character even more for her spirited words to Mr. Rochester when she says,

"I am no bird; and no net ensnares me. I am a free human being with an independent will," she tells him.

Like Jane, we want freedom and independence and it hasn't always been easy. Sometimes we have broken the rules, and gone against tradition or social mores. Sometimes we've caved. But our greatest joy has come when we have been true to that which resides in all of us: the need for love, the need to believe (or not to believe), the need to find our place in the world—needs that are often driven by the vagaries of the human heart. We wouldn't have it any other way.

The Self I Left Behind

Lillian Lindy

The most important lesson I ever learned was how to become me.

I was raised to be a wife and mother. My father, while not strict, was a difficult man, and I learned to obey my parents at all times. When I was seventeen years old, I met a young man, Serge, and fell like a ton of bricks. When we learned that he was not Jewish, my father forbade me to see him again. I did see him one more time to say goodbye, but that was it. I was devastated, but I was such a sycophant that I could not imagine disobeying my father's command.

I went from father to husband, as was usual in that generation. In those days, if you reached the age of twenty-one and were not married, you were considered to be an old maid. I married at the age of nineteen. In my twelve year marriage, I was the compliant one, always agreeing with my husband, rarely expressing my opinion. I defended him when he was in the wrong, even though I felt disdain for his behavior. As the marriage deteriorated, I felt quite lost. I was alone with no family members anywhere around me. Shortly before my divorce, I started to find my own voice with the help of a psychiatrist.

After my divorce, I realized that I did not know "me," but I did know that I had to rebuild my psyche. I had to learn to cope with matters that I have never coped with before like painting a wall or fixing a leaky faucet. I had to get a credit

A Step in the Right Direction

card in my own name since I had no credit rating of my own. What a life lesson that was! I fought tooth and nail with the credit card company. Finally they agreed to issue me one for a limited amount. It was only when I remarried and wanted to change the name on the card that I learned the reason for the limitation. It was because the law at that time made a husband responsible for his wife's debts.

I was livid when the woman told me that the good credit rating I had managed to maintain for four years was for naught. She didn't stop there.

She said, "Think of it this way. It's a good life lesson."

I wanted to scream when she said that, but instead I looked at her and thought to myself how I would love to teach her a life lesson or two.

You don't get to be a whole person or independent when you have been dependent on someone for the first thirty years of your life, so becoming "me" took some time. Trust me, I have never been dependent on anyone in my life since then. Whether or not the real me is good or bad, I can't say. But I am finally a woman who feels good about herself. It took me quite awhile, but it happened, and I am glad.

I feel so strongly to this day that every young woman needs to live independently and start a career before she commits to a serious relationship. I learned this lesson the hard way. Then I found Sandy, my second husband, who for the next 38 years was my equal, loving partner.

Lessons Learned

Nancy Mather

My husband Steve died in 1970 and I became a working mother. It was a turn of events I had never dreamed would occur. I soon realized that I would need to get a job if I was to succeed in my role as a working mother. I would need to come up with an idea to make it work. I decided to compartmentalize my responsibilities: caring for my children, succeeding at work, keeping myself together. It was the beginning of a career in banking. It was also the beginning of a new life where all decisions were left to me with no need for approval. I was now on my own, though there were times when I was fortunate enough to have support from my family and friends.

I got a job at Hartford National Bank and Trust Co. The manager of the bank's branch where I began to work as a teller took me aside one day after I'd been working at the branch a couple of months.

"Nancy, you have more to offer than working as a teller. I will see to your training so you can work as a Personal Banking Representative and move you to the head office."

From that position at the head office I moved to the Marketing Division. The manager there gave me a job as a bank ombudsman. I had mixed feelings about this since it entailed visiting the bank's branches throughout the state pretending to be a customer and reporting my findings back to management. At times my findings were negative so I

A New Kind of Busy

would joke about being the Mata Hari of HNB. My favorite job was when I became Director of Special Events. In that role I hosted meetings and dinners, and was responsible for creating the setting at branch openings. I had a great time in that role except for the time when I organized a branch opening at the Hartford's new Civic Center. I invited the Governor's Guard dressed in full regalia to attend that opening as well as the then Mayor of Hartford to read a proclamation I had composed complete with gold seal and ribbon. One can imagine that my embarrassment was seared in my memory when upon reading it he turned to me and said:

"You call this a proclamation?"

However, there was a better scene at the grand opening of the Landmark Square Branch in Stamford where after the Mayor gave his speech and cut the ribbon, a steel band struck up its music and the assembled group of onlookers erupted into applause. A far better memory.

There were other rewards, too. It brought me, a widow with a limited social life, into a world of dinner parties and other events where I dressed in evening gowns, created menus with the chef, arranged place and table settings, hired musicians and mingled with top executives of the bank along with the top community and business leaders of the time. It is said that nothing remains the same and it was at my next job, one of my last positions at the bank, as Manager of a Financial Counseling Service, that I learned something important that I hadn't known, at least consciously – that I really love meeting people and enjoy public speaking.

What I didn't love about that job was when I felt as if I was

In My Element

beating my head against the wall. As I tried to convince Sr. Management of the value of this service, a public relations product that would bring in new customers, I also did the job and achieved results. Or those evenings when driving home I would evaluate what was happening in my other compartments. How were my kids doing, were they keeping up with their school work, was my job depriving me from spending time with them, was I there for them when they needed me and was I keeping up with all that was essential.

One day, I received a call, out of the blue, from a woman telling me she had read Steve's obituary, and having recently lost her husband, empathized with what I was going through. She asked if I was seeking help, needed someone to talk to. She then went on,

"There is a Catholic Priest I highly respect who offers Pastoral Counseling and had helped me through the loss of my husband."

I never heard from her again after receiving that call. I sometimes wonder what happened to her. I think of the priest Father Kiley whom she had recommended and from whom I had sought advice. How well he helped me throughout that time. I think of him, together with my sister Ann and her husband Tom, as guardian angels who were there for me when I needed support.

In spring of 1978 I met the man who was to become my second husband, Walter Mather, a brilliant attorney and a divorced father of nine grown children, who swept me off my feet. In 1980 Walter and I married. I was once again a wife, now with a large family and a loving generous husband. Walter had many eclectic interests and accomplishments. He had an interest in home décor and had a wonderful tasteful collection of antiques so I gave him carte blanche to make my home ours. Before long he turned it into a beautiful welcoming place for family and friends. We had shared interests so there were plays, operas, concerts and lectures we attended which enriched our life. We would go off on fun weekend excursions to antiques shops where we would search for interesting decorative objects. We entertained family and friends at dinner parties and holidays. All sadly came to an end when Walter was diagnosed with Alzheimer's disease. With a heavy heart I witnessed my beautiful husband lose himself bit by bit along with his power of speech. No longer able to care for him at home I was persuaded to place him in a nursing home where he died in 2014.

Here I am ten years shy of a century. Once again, I have the freedom to come and go as I please, to make my own decisions and make my remaining years count. Since 1994, I have been an active member of the University of Hartford Presidents' College. During my years as a retiree I have loved being in a classroom among my peers where wonderful teachers lead us in animated discussions of the liberal arts. 🌱

Union 101

Bette Marafino

❝Don't jingle your keys or tap your fingers while at a faculty meeting.❞

My husband, Ray, said this on the day of my first faculty meeting as a full-time instructor at Tunxis Community College. He had seen this behavior at too many of his own faculty meetings at another campus to prompt this comment. Though I'm not one to always follow his directions, this one I took to heart – well, maybe too much to heart.

Prior to my time at Tunxis, I had been content to be quiet and compliant at meetings, but when I landed in the Tunxis English department, I became a more active participant.

Maybe it was because the college was in its infancy or because the number of faculty and professional staff were few. It was exciting to be a part of a new beginning.

In addition to committee and faculty meetings, the college instituted a Faculty Association and a separate Professional Staff Association. We knew from day one that trouble was afoot. In an effort to bolster student enrollment, the college President and Academic Dean advertised courses that, though they sounded intellectually exciting on paper, had not been developed or approved by any Academic Standards committee. *World War I*, *Paradise Lost*, and *The American Indian* were a few that fell into this category. Students attempting to register were told those courses were not available, causing upset and anger and prompting students to

I Find My Niche

visit the Academic Dean's office and hold a sit-in.

Fearing that this negative publicity would put our college in a very bad light, we decided to take action. I still don't know how this happened, but I found myself the leader of the Faculty Association and spokesperson for the faculty. A vote of no confidence in the President and Academic Dean was signed by a majority of the faculty and professional staff. At the time of this action, no one had tenure and the state had not yet instituted collective bargaining or union recognition. Were we vulnerable? Most definitely.

But it is still one of the proudest moments of my academic career.

After the no confidence vote, four of us were appointed to write a white paper. This sixty page document detailed all the unsound practices of the administration and received notice by the media. Jon Sablon, then a reporter for NBC, Channel 30, visited the campus, knocked on my classroom door, and when I opened it, his camera started recording my answer to his question.

"Do you want the President to resign?"

Unnerved by his sudden appearance, I stumbled through the question, but did manage to say,

"Yes. He should resign."

Months later we four authors were summoned to the Board of Trustees meeting where we presented our white paper and spoke to our grave concerns about the fate of the college. Bob Vater, who taught at another community college in the system and later became the first President of the community college union, met us at the entrance to the Board room, and rubbing his hands together in delight, said,

Working With Congressman John Larson

"You people have big balls."

Yet another proud moment for me.

This resulted in the Board of Trustees denying the college President and Academic Dean their annual salary increase and both our Faculty and Professional Staff Associations were declared "unofficial." One year later the President resigned followed six months later by the Academic Dean. At the college we formed a united Professional Staff Organization (PSO) which exists to this day.

And what happened to us? A few years later, one of the white paper writers became the Chancellor of the Connecticut Community College system and the three of us continued to teach at Tunxis. I became active in the 4C's – the community colleges union – and served as its president for six years. I often recount this story to younger faculty to show that it's important to stand up for what is fair and right rather than just grouse about it. Nothing like "strength in numbers." ❧

I Am My Mother's Daughter

Ketti Marks

It was a beautiful day for graduation. My colleagues and I were waiting for the head of security to open the lobby doors. We needed to be at our posts before the parents arrived. All of a sudden, an officious-looking young man appeared.

He said, "Follow me and I'll let you in."

He guided us around to the back of the building and up some steps before he disappeared. We found ourselves on a near-dark backstage. We were walking carefully in our suits and dresses and heels because the floor was strewn with bits of scenery. Eventually, we made our way down. Our erstwhile guide was smiling at us from the back of the empty auditorium. Behind him, an empty lobby loomed, and its doors to the outside were wide-open.

I was furious, and the fact that he looked so pleased with himself only made me more furious. As I walked down the long center aisle of the auditorium, I looked straight at him. Finally, when I was just a foot or less away, I said,

"Are you out of your f...ing mind?"

Most of the time, though, I rebel quietly. A few years ago, I was at an RPI fraternity dinner. The Master of Ceremonies asked everyone to stand for a toast to the President. Everyone did, except for me. I couldn't bring myself to stand for Donald Trump.

I don't regret my words to that self-satisfied young man that long-ago June day; I don't regret sitting while a hundred other

It's in the Genes!

people rose. I was being true to myself, and that is a lesson my mother taught me well; a lesson that came to life for both of us during my *get*, or Jewish divorce.

The week before the *get*, the rabbi had called and asked my mother for her Hebrew name.

"I don't have one," she said.

"May I speak to your husband?"

"He's not here, and he doesn't have one, either."

From my perch on the couch across the narrow living room, I smiled. Of course my parents had Hebrew names. And my father? He was happily puttering away in the basement, oblivious to what was going on upstairs. I knew that my mother, who was a devout atheist, just wanted to give the rabbi a hard time.

On the day of the ceremony, I wore a dress I usually reserved for open school nights when I wanted to look especially teacherly: long sleeves, modest neckline, hem below the knee. Perfect for rabbis. One last look in the mirror and I was ready. My mother and I took the D train into Manhattan. Soon, I was in a dim room, standing in front of three solemn and bearded men, all in black suits and immaculate white shirts.

A rabbi handed me a document and said, "Repeat after me."

I repeated his words, my fingers holding tight to the page. He continued reading.

"Blessed are you, your infinite power, Majesty of the Universe, who free those who are bound..."

My eyes flashed. I felt the tension boiling up inside. "I'm not going to say that!"

"Just say it," he said, looking at me wearily.

Finally, the ritual was over. David had his *get*, and I had what I wanted—I would be clear of his debts. An even exchange.

In the outer room, there were more rabbis, and my mother gave them one of her little lectures.

"You know," she said, "a civil divorce should be enough for you. This isn't Israel; it's the United States."

I stood by silently, watching and listening, like I usually do. Then we headed for the elevator, the rabbis' soft voices echoing behind us. Once we were back outside we breathed a mutual sigh of relief. I looked at my watch. One o'clock. Perfect. Time for lunch.

"See that coffee shop over there," I said, "the one with the green sign? Let's go get a BLT."

My little rebellion. I love BLTs, especially when they pile on the bacon, a definite 'no-no' in the Orthodox community.

As we made our way to the coffee shop, I wondered if I'd get my typewriter back from David's brother Ezra in time to do next week's lesson plans. So far, he had refused to return it, but last night my mother had called him and issued one of her ultimatums. As usual, she had been blunt, telling him,

"If we don't get that typewriter back tonight, I will be outside Coney Island Hospital tomorrow morning telling everyone the doctor is a thief."

I knew she would do exactly as she had promised. After all, she had testified against her father in court. She wouldn't hesitate to call out a penny-pinching, humorless hypocrite like David's brother. He was doing the wrong thing, and my mother wasn't going to let him get away with that.

I still remember my first lesson in doing the right thing. It happened when I was six. Gwen and Judy were my two best friends on Bergen Street. Judy wasn't coming to my birthday party even though Gwen was.

"Why isn't she coming?" I asked.

My mother, a nurse who adored babies and children of all colors, stopped ironing and said slowly, "Judy's mother is from the South and won't let her play with Negroes."

I nodded, absorbing the information.

Years later, true to form, she supported my sister's decision to go on a Freedom Ride. When it was my turn to protest, Vietnam this time, my mother thought that was the right thing to do, too, and she supported me, just like she had supported my sister. She had one proviso, though.

"You're not riding the subway in the middle of the night. Your father will drive you." she said.

"He doesn't have to do that," I said.

"Yes, he does," my mother replied.

And that was the end of that. Inside, I was relieved. I really didn't want to be alone on the subway before dawn. But I wouldn't admit that, not then.

She was always on guard, ready for the next wrong action. One day, when I was seventeen, we were in the garment district. Two young men suddenly appeared at my side, smiling and ready to pounce. My mother catapulted over. They took one look at her, and went on their way. When she was eighty, I had an altercation with a man in the grocery store. In my peripheral vision I could see my mother's arms stiffen and her face tighten into an alabaster mask. It was eerie. She looked like she was succumbing to rigor mortis.

When it was over and we were outside, I said, "What would you have done if he had gotten physical?"

She looked down at her hand and curled her fingers into a fist. Then she looked up at me, her green-hazel eyes sparking with intent and said,

"I was getting ready to smash those glasses into that fat face of his."

"Right," I said. I took her arm, and we walked home.

If anyone had heard our conversation outside the grocery store, they had probably been thinking to themselves, "that's one hard cookie." But I knew better. I smiled to myself, as an image from the past played out in my head.

It is winter, and I am sleeping in the little bed that my father built. My mother comes into my room and gently strokes my forehead.

"Ketti, wake up, it's time to get ready for school," she whispers.

I stir, all sleepy, and soon I am snuggling inside her warm blue robe, and we walk downstairs together, one sure step at a time, ready to start our new day.

Many years have passed now, and the *get* is buried deep in my files. But I still think about a long ago morning when my mother and I stood defiant before the rabbis, fire in our eyes. I think, too, about something that happened when I was twenty-five and living in my little studio in Queens.

"I've met someone new," I announced to my mother over the phone.

"Who?" she asked.

"Guess," I said, smiling to myself.

She didn't miss a beat. Like most mothers, she had the list memorized. After her fifth try, she gave up. I told her.

"He's a rabbi," I said.

There was a pregnant pause.

"Well, I'll be goddamned!"

I laughed, and understood her response. I'm not sure those rabbis would have. 🌱

"I go, I go; look how I go…"
Puck in A Midsummer's Night Dream

CHAPTER 4

Away

At different points in our lives we decided to say good-bye to a person, a place, or a comfort zone. Sometimes the break was permanent, sometimes it was temporary, but it was always our choice, whether that meant rejecting a person we had allowed to hurt us, or traveling to a place we hadn't been before, either metaphorically or physically. At critical junctures, we dared to explore.

Travel With the Lindys

Lillian Lindy

W e decided we wanted to visit Japan. I was so excited because I had always been fascinated with Japanese culture and art, and this was my opportunity to be up close and personal with it.

My husband had mileage with United Airlines, so we flew first class from Hartford to Tokyo. What a way to fly!! On the flight, while I was sleeping, a drunken passenger fell on me. I screamed and the flight attendants came to my rescue. What an auspicious way to start a trip!!

Arriving in Tokyo, a city reminiscent of New York with skyscrapers and lots of people, we checked into our hotel where we were staying on the 35th floor. Sandy was not well, and slept for the next 24 hours. I decided I needed to get out of the hotel room, so I left to walk around. Everything was written in Japanese; therefore I could not read anything. After about an hour I began to feel uncomfortable in that environment, so I returned to the hotel and watched Sumo wrestling on television. Westerners tend to laugh when they see two obese men wearing very little clothing try to throw their opponent out of a small circle of space. However, after watching intently for a while, I realized there was a strategy to this sport. The idea is to catch your opponent off balance and then throw him out of the circle. It isn't necessarily the biggest contender who wins the match.

Finally Sandy was well enough to explore Tokyo. One of

the first things we noticed was how clean the city was. There was no litter anywhere. Taxi cab drivers wore white gloves and cleaned their cars while waiting for fares. We visited temples and passed by the Emperor's palace. We saw beautiful gardens everywhere we went. I was struck by the simplicity of these gardens in which one flower with one sprig of green made for a beautiful presentation. As we continued our tour of the city, we encountered the hotel designed by Frank Lloyd Wright, which was the only building left standing after a severe earthquake hit Tokyo in 1923. Wright's concept of rollers would allow walls and roofs to sway with the earth's motion. What a genius!

We ate American breakfasts, as I need a jolt of coffee in the morning, and traditional Japanese breakfasts serve Miso soup and lord knows what else. Eating in Japan was a challenge, but except for breakfast we wanted to eat like the Japanese. So we started going into local restaurants where a waiter would hand us a menu with the word menu printed on the outside cover. However, when we opened the menu, everything was in Japanese. We soon learned that we could order our meal from the plastic replicas displayed in the window of the restaurant. We would let a waiter know we were there and then he would meet us outside. All we had to do was point to the replica of the dish that we wanted. We ate extremely well. Desserts are not a part of the Japanese cuisine, but we discovered that the latest rage in Tokyo was coffee houses. I could have coffee and my husband could have dessert.

One day, Sandy said he wanted to ride the Japanese subway, but after having seen pictures of "pushers" who

For a Moment the World Lay Still at My Feet

literally pushed people into the subway cars, I was hesitant, but I agreed to do it. That night after dinner, we entered the subway station. Once again, everything was in Japanese, and you had to buy a ticket to your destination. A young man saw our distress, and helped us. It was well after nine at night, and the subway was quite crowded; however, it was not in need of pushers.

We went to Kamakura by train to see what is probably the largest Buddha in the world. From there we traveled by Shinkansen, the bullet train, to Kyoto. What a beautiful city, peaceful and filled with unusual temples and Tori gates. We toured just about every temple there was. One temple really stood out for us. It had an open space that was filled with white pebbles and brownish stones, some large and some small. You could imagine islands in a sea, mountain tops over the clouds; anything or everything. I could have stayed there for a very long time. It was the most peaceful place I have ever been to or seen.

After leaving one temple, and on our way to another one, I had to go to the bathroom. We stopped by our hotel where I remembered there was a bathroom in the lobby. I entered, and there was one western toilet and one eastern. An eastern toilet is very clean, but essentially a hole in the ground. I waited for the western toilet, but the person was not departing, so I used the eastern toilet. When I came out, a Japanese woman came out of the western toilet. I laughed, and she looked at me and she laughed too.

Soon we decided we wanted to have a more authentic experience and moved to a hotel which had a traditional Japanese flavor. In our room we noticed there was no furniture, and no place to put your suitcase. Very simple and unadorned. That evening, a housekeeper knocked on the door and put a futon and rice pillows on the floor for us. Rice pillows are as hard as rocks, but amazingly comfortable as they let in air and really support your head and neck. We started joking about the futon and sang *Stomping at the Savoy*. We made up a crude expression about the futon. It began with an F. We also had a traditional Japanese bath in the bathroom. The rule is to wash before getting into the bath. The water is blazingly hot, and believe me, when you get out of this bath, you just want to sleep, as it is so relaxing!

In these smaller cities, my husband received quite a lot of attention, given his beard and handlebar mustache. Japanese men are mostly devoid of facial hair. So Sandy's hirsute face was quite an attraction. Children would go up to him and run their hands over his face. In one garden, a woman approached us, and with body language and a camera asked if she could take his picture. Sandy certainly enjoyed being the center of attention.

I will never forget the hours I spent at The Peace Park in Hiroshima which had been built as a somber reminder of the atomic bomb that fell on Hiroshima toward the end of WWII. The cenotaph stands in ruined form as a symbol of the destruction of this city. The Park's museum uses dioramas to show the bombing, and the effect it had on human beings who had to endure skin falling off their still live bodies. At the entrance to the museum there was a sign in English which indicated that there had been no warning about the bomb. That was contrary to everything I had heard before. We looked around and saw many Japanese visitors, and I wondered, *Do they know I am an American? Do they hate me?* However, I did not sense any animosity. At the end of our visit, Sandy said that whenever a peace conference was to be held, it should take place at this site in Hiroshima. When we left the Peace Park, I was feeling perplexed as to whether we did the right thing or not in the bombing of Hiroshima and Nagasaki.

We wanted to get a good view of Mt. Fujiyama, which is revered by the Japanese. It is an impressive volcano/ mountain. So we undertook a trip to Moto Hakone. It was an uplifting experience after Hiroshima.

In Moto Hakone, we stayed at a Japanese hotel for two nights. We learned that breakfast and dinner would be served in our rooms. The room was very sparsely furnished. There was a very low table in the center where we would eat our meals. At the appointed hour, a woman came in with food and cooking utensils and started to prepare our dinner. I had my trusty English-Japanese dictionary, and between this woman, the dictionary, and body language we managed to communicate. We learned she had a young daughter about age seven. My husband had brought emblems with him depicting the US, and gave the woman an emblem for her daughter.

On our second afternoon we decided to return to our hotel and take advantage of its "Spa" which was a huge Japanese bath, more like a stream. There was one bath for women and one for men. I opened the door and soon I was walking nude and trying to cover myself as much as possible with a towel the size of a washcloth. I had always thought I was small-busted, but I felt like Jayne Mansfield after seeing the

Japanese women. I washed completely before getting into the bath, sitting on the bottom of a bucket. When I got up, I had a rim mark on my "tush" and the ladies smiled. This bath was like a small pool, the water was very warm, and thoroughly delightful. I did not want to get out.

My husband was enjoying his men's spa when he was approached by a man who didn't speak English. The man was pointing to his upper arm, trying very hard to communicate with him. Sandy figured out that the man was trying to say thank you for the emblem we had given to his daughter. That evening, when the woman came to prepare our dinner, she brought a small note printed in English which her daughter had written, thanking us for the emblem. People all over the world can really be lovely.

Back to Tokyo where on one of our last mornings we got up at five o'clock to visit the Tokyo fish market. We were amazed. It looked like the entire Pacific Ocean had been drained of fish. There were fish we had never seen before, and huge tunas with their heads and tails chopped off lying flash frozen on the floor. Sushi anyone!!! It was an incredible sight.

I have traveled extensively, but none of my other trips were as fascinating as my trip to Japan. I will never forget the gardens, the architecture, or the traditional female attire. Most of all, I will never forget those times when my senses seemed more awake, drawn as they were to the simplicity and sensuality of the Japanese aesthetic. I would go back in a flash.

A Journey of Discovery

Nancy Mather

I had traveled with my late husband Steve to Italy, and after he died I vividly remember thinking my dream of travel was over, never again would I have that opportunity. But I did and the world opened up to me.

In 1972, I decided to take my children to Europe to celebrate my elder son Stephen's graduation from high school. We toured England, France, and Switzerland, traveling to cities their father had visited and where we would meet some of his business associates. It proved to be the right thing to do for the right reasons. We have wonderful memories of that trip. On a bus trip through the Loire Valley we met two very prim American women, retired school teachers who, of all things, convinced me that I should take my children to the Folies Bergére. One Saturday evening, dressed for the occasion, we went to the theatre along with a friend and her two children. At the theatre we entered the lobby filled with theatregoers and created a bit of a stir. Here were two women with five children of various ages to see a performance known to be risqué. One can imagine the raised eyebrows of the theatregoers. One afternoon my friend and I went to the Galleries Lafayette leaving my daughter Nancy Ellen with her brothers in charge. We returned to the hotel to find Stephen and Robert frantically looking for their missing sister. We finally found her after quite some time in the H.Stern Jewelry Store, chatting with the saleswomen about

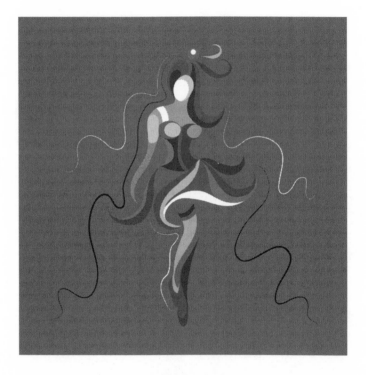

OOH LA LA!

her rock collection.

In 1978 an opportunity for more exotic travel came my way. I went to Pakistan, a country Steve had visited on business. After a long flight I deplaned at a small airport in Islamabad, the capital. It was a brilliant sunny day. Soon I was walking into a small courtyard where a man was bent over sweeping with a small bundle of twigs. In a corner a group of men were talking. They were wearing turbans and the shalwar kameez, a loose tunic over baggy trousers which I soon learned was the national dress of Pakistan. It was a scene straight out of *National Geographic.* I can still see the fuchsia pink bougainvillea surrounding white stucco homes, and I remember, too, the wonderful scent of jasmine that drifted in the windows as I was driven to the home of my hosts.

My hosts, Sunny and Afsal Khan had been business associates of Steve. They warmly welcomed me and asked how I felt after such a long flight and about my overnight stay in London. They showed me to a bright and airy beautifully appointed bedroom to freshen up. At dinner we discussed their plans during the length of my visit. It was clear they wished me to get to know their country and so they made arrangements for me to be taken to the key cities of Karachi, Lahore, and Peshawar, among others.

I loved my morning ritual when a young maid entered my bedroom and asked would I like a massage after breakfast. How could I ever refuse such a luxury? A simple breakfast of chapati, a small flat bread, along with fruit and tea were served, after which I had my massage, and so began my first morning in Islamabad. Later I went off to Rawalpindi, a city

Getting Around Islamabad

close to Islamabad with two young American women college classmates of one of the Khan daughters. There I was transported to a different world. Street signs were printed in Arabic script, and buses painted in colorful designs were crowded with men hanging from open windows and sitting on the roof as the bus moved along. We walked along a street lined with stores that looked more like stalls because of their wide-open entrances. As we passed by, the colorful wares in the shops were visible and created a colorful scene. There were fruit, vegetable and spice vendors, along with other shops selling comestibles and beautiful silks for saris. Many of the women shopping wore saris, while others wore chadors, the loose-fitting black outfits which completely cover them from head to toe. Men walked about in the traditional outfit of shalwar chemise though few were in western dress. It was a fascinating eye-opening day which gave us a chance to see a slice of the everyday life of the inhabitants.

Another time the two college women and I went to Lahore where we spent two nights. It was then and is today a thriving city, the largest of the Punjab Province. It has interesting historic landmarks dating back to the Mughal era of the seventeenth century. We were fortunate to visit two of the most wondrous landmarks from that era. We entered the Badshahi Mosque which was awe-inspiring due to the sheer breadth of its halls and pillars. It is a huge, deep red building with a tall Minaret (tower) from which a Muezzin calls worshipers to prayer. We then visited the Shalimar Mughal Gardens known for its sheer beauty of design. That evening we went to a large meeting where a turbaned bearded man dressed in long robes held court. He called out to people sitting in the audience, speaking in Urdu. At one point he picked me out of the audience and speaking in English asked where I came from and out of the blue said I would one day have something published. A year later an article I had written relative to my work was published. I wondered had I been in the presence of a Seer when in Lahore.

The time in Peshawar, the capitol of a Pakistani province, proved to be my most memorable experience. One of my hosts took me on a drive along the Khyber Pass, the road leading from Peshawar to Kabul in Afghanistan. As we drove along the road, there were signs of the time when the British occupied the territory. I saw British Insignias cut into the huge rocks that lay at the base of high hills. At the top of these remnants of abandoned British forts were still standing. It was like traveling through the pages of Rudyard Kipling's *Kim*. Today, the Pass is a free territory and governed by tribal law. The tribal men carry rifles and wear ammunition belts slung over their shoulders and across their chests. They are a handsome lot. They live in homes surrounded by high mud walls. I was reminded of movies I had seen of places like this. Near the end of our drive, we stopped for tea in an old British Club that was long past its glory, another reminder of what had once been.

The day there that really stands out in my memory, because it was so strange, was when we visited a furniture factory. The factory owner impressed me. He invited Sunny and me into his home where he escorted us into a beautiful living room. I thought to myself, he is so cordial.

But as he and Sunny sat chatting, my eyes roamed around the room. There on a table alongside my chair was a framed photo of a man who was dressed in the black uniform of a Nazi SS officer. I realized it was my host, that I was in the chilling presence of a former Nazi.

I can't begin to describe my feelings at that moment as a disturbing thought came to mind. *Was he a Nazi who had somehow gotten away? Was he one of those who had committed horrific crimes?*

Sunny and I left while I was still in a daze. The next day I flew to Karachi from Peshawar on an old prop plane, a German Junker of WWII vintage. Seeing that small old plane made me nervous. My fears were allayed as I watched the passengers come aboard carrying all sorts of things including caged chickens. It became clear this was a regular commuter flight. Sitting in that old WWII German plane turned my thoughts to the furniture factory and the old Nazi I met there. I looked out the window at the dry, dun-colored hills and uninhabitable earth below, and thought that this is where he belonged, not in a beautiful house where he had every luxury money could buy.

Though the view had not been very comforting, it was a smooth flight and we landed safely in Karachi. Upon my arrival I was taken to the home of Sunny's family where that evening I met a number of her relatives. Among them was Sunny's sister with whom I chatted amiably. We were clearly playing "getting to know you." She told me the Karachi shoreline was beautiful.

Before parting she asked, "Would you like to walk along the beach with me tomorrow?"

So the next morning off she and I went, and I saw that the shoreline, with its pale-colored sand and gently lapping waves was indeed beautiful. The beach was empty except for us and three camels grazing in the distance. The camels on the beach on a clear sunny morning is a picture I still carry in my mind along with a comment my companion made as we walked.

She said, "Nancy there is harmony in you."

To this day I wonder what she saw in me, what I could have said to her the night before that would have prompted such an observation, which I took as a compliment.

I had so many wonderful experiences when I traveled to places I could only have imagined visiting when I was a young adult. I am still having wonderful experiences today. I am getting the education I didn't pursue as a young woman. And in 2006, talents I once thought of as dormant were called upon when I was asked to coordinate and chair the Presidents' College Volunteer Program. This year, with the start-up of a Presidents College Speakers Bureau, I find I'm drawing upon skills I first became aware of all those years ago when I was driving across Connecticut to speak to community groups about banking.

I now live alone. My children are grown, married and successful. I have five young adult grandchildren of whom I am very proud. I recently gave my youngest grandson, who is in his senior year in college, these words to live by: "Always keep an open heart and mind as you make your way through life."

Westward Ho!

Bette Marafino

Taking a cross country trip in the summer of 2012 with my son Andy and 16-year-old grandson Brian was a spur of the moment thing for me and a chance to live out of the bubble.

With Andy and his family living in Southern California, I had flown over the country many times, but this was my first trip by car. So, when Andy asked me if I wanted to go with them, I didn't hesitate. I'm an easterner at heart and once we left that part of the country there were many surprises as we headed to California.

We set off the last week in July and had very hot weather throughout the trip. Because we love baseball, there was a baseball theme to our trip. Our first baseball stop was in Louisville, Kentucky, to visit the Louisville Slugger factory/ museum. It was interesting to see a piece of wood transformed into a baseball bat for a professional ball player. In this case it was for the Yankees Nick Swisher. That night we made a stop in St. Louis to see a Cardinals game. The stadium was packed with red shirts, caps and all things red as the fans suffered through the hot sticky weather to cheer on their "red birds."

Then it was on to Oklahoma. From the road I called my sister, who had always wanted to visit the state. Her vision of Oklahoma was from the Gordon MacRae movie musical of the same name where the "corn is as high as an elephant's

There's More to a Bat Than a Piece of Wood

eye." The scorching heat and lack of rain had left the corn plants brown and droopy. They were about as high as an elephant's ankle.

We weren't too far into that state when we discovered that one of our rear tires was going flat. The "Welcome to Oklahoma" attendant at the rest stop told us to take the next exit to Miami, Oklahoma. It was upon entering Miami that I felt I was in a very different world. Located on the old historic Route 66, a drive down the main street showed a town that belonged in the 1950s. Old storefronts, most of which needed a new coat of paint, included the post office, Dollar store and an assortment of bars. We pulled into a shabby looking gas station that advertised "Tires for Sale." The gas station office was filthy and the shop's owner, Ray, welcomed us with a friendly,

"Hi, can I hep you folks?"

Ray was casual with his feet up on the desk, a Bud and a cigarette in hand as the fan above his head whirred and made the nearby bug-filled fly paper flutter in the breeze.

"Have a seat, little lady," said Ray as he motioned me to the couch over by the dirty window.

The greased-stained couch did not look inviting, but I didn't want to offend, so I sat in an erect position with my butt barely touching the cushion while Andy and Brian opted to stand. While we waited for Ray's "guy" to come back from McDonald's, Ray chatted about the hot weather and said we didn't "talk like folks around here." A young boy walked through the office and into the garage.

"That's my boy," said Ray. "I call him Whiskey."

" How old is your son?" I asked.

I Was There!

"Oh, he's 11," said Ray. And a voice from the garage yelled,

" I'm thirteen, Dad."

Andy and Brian shot me a quick look and I could see they were trying to stifle their laughter. While we waited, another customer came into the office, The best way to describe him was to think of Santa Claus in denim overalls. Ray and this guy talked about the rodeo which had just been in town and agreed that the bull riding was the best. Ray's guy came back from lunch and was unable to give us the needed tire for the 1990 Honda. We were directed to the local Walmart where we spent a few hours in the air-conditioned store while our new tire was put on the car. Now we were off to Tulsa.

Before we got to Tulsa we stopped for lunch at the mecca for all gourmands – The Golden Corral – which featured its famous all-you-can-eat buffet. The commercials are correct. You can help yourself to everything from leafy salad greens to a juicy steak with all the fixins. The dessert bar was about a mile long with a rotating chocolate fountain as the centerpiece. Andy, Brian and I indulged in fried chicken, mashed potatoes, molasses-spiked pork ribs and, oh yes, we grabbed some marshmallows and fruit and plunged them into the chocolate fountain.

Then we were off to Tulsa. We were stopping in Tulsa to see the Tulsa Drillers, a farm team of the Colorado Rockies. Andy had been a baseball coach at Bishop Montgomery High School in Torrance, California, and one of his former players, Mike Zuanich was now on the Drillers. He knew we were coming and had reserved free tickets. When we arrived in Tulsa, the weather sign on the bank said 112 degrees at

5:00 o'clock in the afternoon. I dipped my toes in the hotel's outdoor pool and found the water to be bath water hot, so much for a swim. Because of the heat, I decided to stay in the hotel while Andy and Brian went to the game. Later Andy said that though the admission was free, he spent about $30.00 on bottled water.

The rest of our trip was uneventful. As we continued west through Texas, New Mexico, and Arizona, and on into California, the topography changed dramatically. The dry, dusty plains of Oklahoma gave way to a topography that was stark, rocky, and majestic. Variegated rock formations in shades of brown, yellow and pink were framed by a blue sky that seemed huge. It was so different from the parts of the country we had previously passed through. We traveled for miles without seeing any buildings or people.

I often think fondly of this trip and would like to do it again, only this time taking a more northern route. ❦

Out of the Bubble

Ketti Marks

I broke out of the Lenny bubble in 2009. I had been enmeshed in my cage for thirty-five years, and although every decade or so I peeped through the tangles, I never really got free. Not until the last time. It was spring, and I was living on East 94th Street and 3rd Avenue in Manhattan when I got the e-mail.

"Will you meet me for coffee?" he asked.

I wanted to shut the computer, but I didn't. I wanted to delete the web address that always gave me a pang, but I didn't. I answered, and we met at the Barnes and Noble across from Union Square. We were both into books, of course, but that wasn't why we met there. It was neutral territory, peopled by like souls, and for me, noncommittal, even though I always left committed. And so I saw him again.

Those first few weeks we talked about Obama, and how we had both cried when he'd been elected. He read to me from his latest novel and opined on Philip Roth, his favorite New York writer. But he was different. His perfect white teeth had turned yellow-brown and his eyes, his narrow brown eyes that used to be so intense and vibrant had dulled into sad reflections of a dissipated life.

It all started years before in the faculty lounge at Brooklyn College where we were both adjuncting. That first day is so clear in my mind. No discordant notes, just conversation, the gist of which escapes me today because the substance

Breaking Free

probably wasn't very important, even then. But there was a magnet that seemed to extend in front of me, drawing me across to this fat, smiling stranger with the sexy eyes. After a few minutes, I knew he was different; he didn't conform, and I liked that, child of the '50s and early '60s that I was, when to be different was to be suspect. And I was different. None of my friends had fathers who had ridden the rails during the Depression. Or parents who didn't go to temple on Rosh Hashanah and Yom Kippur. God forbid.

That first day, we put his bicycle in my car and went to a Chinese restaurant for lunch. A few days later we sat on the grass outside his office. He told me that I reminded him of the dark-haired girl running down the road at the beginning of *Mash*. He told me his first book had just been published.

"What's it about?" I asked.

I was curious, but more than that I was happy, just sitting there in the sunshine with him with the whole afternoon before us. That night, I read his novel from cover to cover. Sometimes I ask myself if that was when I got hooked, captivated by him, inexorably so, like I had never been by anyone before.

A few months after we had met, I knocked on his door. He was expecting me.

"Hi," he said, smiling. "Come in and meet Robin."

I walked into his apartment and a moment later Robin came out of the bedroom.

That was the day when the sunshine faded. That was the day I should have left, but didn't.

And I soon learned that other women were only part of my problem. That really hit home one summer afternoon when we were sitting on the beach in Coney Island and watching the waves roll in to shore. I swallowed hard and asked,

"If we were both drowning, and you could only rescue one of us, would you rescue me or your book?"

He thought a few minutes and then said quite seriously,

"I guess I would rescue you. I could always write another book."

I was devastated. My stomach caved. Me and his book. Equal objects in his mind. No, not quite equal. He would always be faithful to his writing, but never to me.

My friends could never understand why I was attracted to Lenny, why I wanted to be with someone who was so different from myself, so fat, uninhibited, lewd, rumpled. When my friend Phyllis first met Lenny at his attic apartment on Avenue J in Brooklyn, she focused for a while on his garish silver and purple wallpaper. Then she looked back and forth between the two of us.

Finally she gave an amazed gulp and said, "You and Lenny!"

Sometimes, the fact that I was with Lenny amazed me, too. On the day I passed my M.A. orals, he had gone to a concert at the College where he sat next to one of the professors who had been on my committee that morning. As he told me at dinner later that night, they had quite a conversation. It started with Professor Springman saying that he didn't much like the girl who had taken her orals that day.

"Did you tell him you know me?" I asked.

"Of course," Lenny said, "I told him I'd been lusting after you for years."

I flinched, and wondered if this spicy nugget would make

its way through the Speech Department.

He definitely had a way with words. One day I was in his office at the College. He had a stack of essays on his desk. On the top one he had written in big red letters, "Give me a f… ing break!"

I asked him, "How could you write that?"

He looked at me quizzically and said, "Why not?"

I left in disgust, walking down the stairs of LaGuardia Hall and across campus repeating to myself, almost like a mantra, *It's over, it's over.* But it wasn't.

People talk about chemistry, that indefinable quality that draws people together. We had that, Lenny and I. One warm early July day, after we'd been apart for years, we ran into each other on a street near NYU. He was doing research at the university's library, and I was taking classes so I could qualify to teach that fall. It was sheer happenstance. I still remember the crinkled white and pink dress I was wearing that day and the way my heart pounded when I saw him walking toward me, how I had to catch my breath when we stopped to talk. For a few weeks we were together again. I had a long break between classes and we spent the time eating lunch before going to a dinky little neighborhood hotel. On our last day, when lunch was over, he gave me his news.

"I'm getting married," he said in a low voice, not looking at me. "She's pregnant."

I went silent. Then I said to him, slowly spacing out my words staccato-like, "You're telling me now?"

Inside, I was remembering what he had said to me in a diner once a few years after we met.

"I want to marry you," he had said. "I love you so much,

but I can't be faithful, not even to you."

I left for a while after that last lunch. But he would always call—a month or two later, a year later. He called from the hospital on the day his daughter was born.

"I need to see you," he said in a matter-of-fact voice. "I want to see you. Let me come over. I'll divorce Sheryl. We'll get married."

I couldn't believe he was calling me on this day of all days. I told him he was crazy and hung up the phone.

Time passed. I came home from work one afternoon to find him sitting in front of my door. And so it went. We were together again. We weren't together again.

Fourteen years ago, in a fury, I sent back his book, I sent back his letters. Then two years later the e-mails began. They followed a familiar pattern. He would express his love and contrition and I would express my anger. Then I would melt when I read,

Know that I will love you until I'm too old to love and *As long as we are alive there will be a tie between us that nothing can sever.*

That was in February. A few months later, we met at Barnes and Noble for coffee.

But finally, one late spring day, I realized it was over for the last time. I sat in the comfortable blue recliner in my apartment on East 94th Street and thought about the devil in his eye that had drawn me to him and how much he had appealed to my romantic imagination. I thought about how we used to read passages from *Jane Eyre* in bed. In some ways, I was still that little girl who used to get lost in the pages of her big red fairy-tale book. But Lenny wasn't a bit like the princes I had read about when I was young.

I've been over him for many years now. Sometimes I ask myself why it took me so long to break out of the bubble and then I remember a rainy weekend I spent in Saugerties with my sister. We were taking shelter under the awning of a small corner bookstore. It was just after a break-up and I was crying. My sister walked over to where I was standing.

She asked me in a voice full of despair, "What do you see in him?"

And I had answered, deep in my own despair, "I can talk to him!"

But that isn't enough, and I saw the truth that day in 2009 when I watched him walk away wearing the same limp blue shirt he had worn for the last month. In that moment, I couldn't bear the thought of being with him. I finally understood that he was lost to me and me to him. Yes, I could communicate with him in a way I had never been able to do with other men. But even so, we had always spun in different orbits, and I needed to spin elsewhere. ❧

"A person's mind is everything, really.
Memory is identity. It's you."
Stephen King writing in *Duma Key*

CHAPTER 5

On Our Minds

O scar Wilde once defined memory as the diary that we all carry about with us. In these pages we have chosen to share our memories of war, of struggles in school, of living at a time when to defy established norms was to be ostracized by others. But there were moments of pride and joy and discovery, too. The moment we made a bully shake with anger. The moment we discovered the unique beauty of another country. The moment we found a domestic freedom we hadn't known existed. Finally, the moment from the past that reaches up often to touch our hearts in some special way.

Flying High

Lillian Lindy

G iving someone a piece of my mind is something I have rarely done. By the time I think of what to say, it is hours after I was insulted, hurt or embarrassed, and too late to retort. Also, it is not in my nature to be aggressive, rude or nasty. Sometimes, the only way for me to "give a piece of my mind" is to do it without the person realizing that he has been given a "lashing."

Mr. J was my boss for about six years, and he was the quintessential MCP (more bluntly, he was a male chauvinist pig of the highest order). I was the first female supervisor in his department but, unlike the male supervisors, everything I did had to be scrutinized by him. In his mind, women were not necessarily "people." He thought women were meant to be secretaries. He made my life miserable for all the years I reported to him. It is difficult to give your boss a piece of your mind if you want to keep your job, so I found other ways to harass him and make myself feel good about my job.

We were in Dallas on a business trip and had arrived at the airport early for our flight. I have an American Airlines Club card, so I said, "Why don't we go to the club to wait for our departure?" He agreed, so I approached the desk with my card and indicated that he was my guest. Then Mr. J said, "What should I do?"

I said, "Nothing, I'm taking care of this, so why don't you just sit down in that chair over there?"

I Did It!

Power to woman!!!

Another time we were in San Francisco walking back from dinner. After a few blocks, I realized that we weren't too far from an area known for its strip joints. I said, "I've always wanted to go to a male strip club," and Mr. J sputtered like mad. So I said to him, "You men think nothing of going to a female strip club, why shouldn't a woman go to a male strip club?" He turned red as a beet.

My second jab at his manhood.

On these trips, Mr. J was not very talkative, so I regaled him with stories about the trips I had taken to places like Japan and Russia and Scandinavia. He was envious of all the traveling I had done, so he told me was going somewhere I had never been, Guam.

I said, "Been there, done that." Silently, I thought to myself, *Why would anyone want to go to Guam? There is nothing there.*

This was my way of getting back at him, and it did my soul a lot of good.

A few years later, our department was reorganized, and Mr. J was moved to another area. Essentially, he was demoted. By that time, there was another female supervisor in the department. I guess my years with the company proved that women could be effective. The two of us held hands, and jumped up and down like children with glee at his departure.

My final jab.

Bye, Bye Mr. MCP. 🌷

The View From My Window

Nancy Mather

Remembering my past as I put words on paper has been a novel experience. I've thought back and recalled experiences that have had a big impact on my life. Though I have barely skimmed the surface, what has become clear is that there was a time when I was so preoccupied with the worries and cares of my daily existence that I was oblivious to the events taking place in the outside world. The Vietnam War with all its horrors passed me by because it was during those years that I was living with the fear that my husband would not survive a life-threatening heart attack and that I would be left a widow with three young children to raise. My fear was realized when he died three years later.

My concerns differ today. I'm keenly aware of what is happening in the world. I find things so different now from the way they were in my earlier years. The middle class isn't as stable as when I was working to support my family. Job security barely exists. Advances in technology make it seem as if *1984* is about to arrive. We once had three or four channels that provided news at set times during the evening. Now our eyes and ears are constantly assaulted by a barrage of unsettling news twenty-four hours a day.

What bothers me most of all, though, is that we have a callous administration that seems determined to destroy everything that is good about this country. It is turning back the clock on civil rights, it is denying refugees the right to

There's a World out There!

asylum, it is ignoring scientists who warn us of the dangers of climate change, and it is making a mockery of our constitution.

I do not let all this negativity overwhelm me, however. I think about the past and how America has always fought to keep our democracy strong. I do believe that what is good about our country will ultimately prevail.

I am grateful for the life I have and for the family, faith, and friends that help me endure. It is because of them that my optimism does not waver.

Everything Is Not O.K.
In the Sunshine State
Bette Marafino

Growing up in the '40s and '50s in New Britain, Connecticut and attending public schools, I didn't know much about the Jim Crow laws that were practiced in parts of our country. And so, after graduating from college and heading to Florida with my new husband to teach in the Pinellas County school system in the summer of 1960, I certainly didn't know how that Florida experience would shape my world view.

The 1954 Brown vs Board of Education decision by the Supreme Court unanimously ruled that "racial segregation of children in public schools was unconstitutional." This ruling helped establish the precedent that "separate but equal" was not equal at all.

So it was a shock when I discovered that there were no black children in San Jose Elementary School where I taught third grade. Not only was the school district defying the 1954 ruling, but the education in the "white and colored" schools was certainly not equal.

My third-grade class was in a brand new building with a playground on a grassy plot of land where kids played tether ball, swung on swings, bounced up and down on the seesaw and climbed on the monkey bars. In contrast, the kids in the colored school in town were housed in an old schoolhouse with a tar-paper roof that was positioned so close to the railroad tracks one could see the building shake as the train

Culture Shock!

raced by. A lone tree with a tire swing was the sole piece of equipment on this dirt-patch playground.

Every Friday afternoon our school custodian came into my classroom and all the other classrooms with a cigar or shoe box which I passed around the room so my third graders could put their used crayons in the box. Any broken or blunt crayons were candidates for the box. The *Weekly Readers* were also collected. This collection was taken by the custodian to that school across the tracks.

Teachers at my school drew straws at the beginning of the school year to identify who would decorate the bulletin boards in the school foyer each month. I drew February. Not bad, I thought, for I had pictures and documents of presidents Washington and Lincoln.

I clearly remember the following scenario that day. I'm standing on a little chair outside the principal's office after school putting up my red, white and blue crepe paper streamers. I had just put up my Washington side and was working on the Lincoln side when my principal, a transplant from Alabama, came from his office.

Arms crossed and shaking his head, he said,

"Young lady, the Washington part can stay; the Lincoln part has to go."

Not understanding him, I asked if my letters were crooked. He persisted.

"Young lady, we don't do that down here." "Do what?" I asked.

My question was followed by a lecture that celebrating Lincoln's birthday was not acceptable. That message was really reinforced when there was an all-school assembly celebrating Jefferson Davis' birthday.

I remember coming home that night and saying to my husband,

"We have to get out of here when the school year ends."

He agreed because he was having similar experiences at his elementary school in a nearby town.

During her February school vacation, my sixteen-year-old sister Bernadette came to visit. One night we went to the movies. I don't remember the name of the movie, but what happened that night is still a vivid memory. The main part of the theater was reserved for the white folks and the colored had to sit in the balcony. During the movie my sister had to use the restroom and when she came back to her seat, she was crying.

"The usher yelled at me," she said.

When I asked, she said she went to the water fountain to get a drink. One fountain said "white" and the other said "colored." My sister went to the colored fountain because she wanted to see the color of the water. That's when the usher told her to get away from that fountain and directed her to the white one.

When my husband and I took a nightly walk in our neighborhood, he would yank down the KKK signs on telephones poles that said, *Be A Man. Join the Klan.* Sure enough, the next night those signs would be back up. But pretty soon we wouldn't be there to see them. The day after school let out for the summer, we were on the road back to Connecticut. 🌷

Connections

Ketti Marks

My dog died three years ago this past winter. He had so many homes, my little dappled Doxie. In Brooklyn he lived, pretty much at ease, in a semi-attached brick house near my old high school. In Manhattan, though, he padded around with lowered head, and when the cacophony of shrieking sirens and rumbling trucks was at its worst, his red-blond body would shake until the danger had passed. Outside, he only wanted to come back in, away from the cracked pavement, away from the trees ensconced in their black mesh prisons. He would tug and I would beg,

"Please, Chips, do something!" I would say. It seemed to take forever.

Next to Trump Tower, where my nephew lived, he perked up a bit. He liked the wide sidewalks and the fragrant doggy smells emanating from the Hudson River. There was a café at the end of the pier. He liked those smells, too. But it was at my sister's house in Connecticut where he was happiest for he was truly a country dog, my Chips.

We found him living alone in a green wire cage set in an expanse of pretty green grass. As soon as I saw him, I knew he was mine. I can see him even now – standing ramrod straight on his hind legs, head turning as he follows the flow of his family's words. Or we are outside, walking in the nature preserve near Sheepshead Bay, and he suddenly freezes, hackles rising, because he has seen a rabbit scurry out from

A Heartbeat at My Feet

Holding Him Close

behind the tall marsh grasses.

My little hunter. He was very small when I toted his black and rust-colored carrier into a bathroom stall at a rest stop. I locked the door. I sat down. He began to bark just as I began to tinkle. At the sinks, I apologized profusely but the two other women just said,

"Can we see him?" and so I opened the zipper and they were enchanted.

A few years later, on Broadway, one of those 'ladies who lunch' seemed enthralled by Chips' red-gold color.

"Do you have him highlighted?" she asked.

Only in New York, I thought to myself, but I smiled sweetly and said, "No, he's all natural."

After she left, I looked at Chips and pointed my finger at him.

"You see, that's what happens when you hang out in Manhattan," I told him.

When I moved to Connecticut, Chips was older. His tiny paws slipped on my new wood floors. I got a long pink runner. I got mats. The only time he didn't slip was the night he ran away with the chicken bone. As he circled the dining room table with his trophy, I got a sense of déjà vu. We had done this before, Chips and me, when he was a puppy.

I remember the end, too. The terrible routine of injections that he endured with a tired sigh. The jars of baby food in the refrigerator, pureed chicken only. The last visit to the veterinarian and her words, "How did we miss this?"

And though it seemed hopeless, we asked "Should we hospitalize him?"

And she looked kindly at us and said, "There's a very small

chance. But I would want to know."

So we did the hospital thing. I cradled his little body in my lap. Then two days later, he was gone. I cried. I couldn't bear looking at his bed or bowls so I put them in the basement where I wouldn't see them. I threw out the jars of pureed baby food and the shiny steel nail clippers. I threw out the red leash, the green leash, his collar. I kept throwing out, a bit of bone from under my bed, the Doxie note cards I had bought on impulse. And in the basement, suddenly confronted by his bed and bowls, I cried and then threw them out, too. In the bathroom cabinet I found his used syringes and the new ones, too. I drove to a local vet's office and asked the receptionist if she would dispose of the old needles for me. She smiled, and I handed over the small plastic container. When I gave her the new needles, she thanked me profusely for the donation. I left, grateful to her, more grateful than she could possibly have been to me.

Two weeks after Chips died, I met Oliver at a mall in Northampton. Oliver was a long-haired dachshund from California who, at the moment, was missing his mother. But as soon as she and her packages appeared, Oliver perked up, gave me a doggy smile, and licked my proffered hand.

It's been three years now, but I still miss Chips. Sometimes he drove me crazy, but mostly he made me happy. He wasn't much for adventure or car rides but he was a great one for snuggling. He especially loved burrowing under the blankets and sharing my pillow. And he had a great sense of self. Once he barked furiously at the garbage can until I gave him back his toy. He was right. How could I, a human, know when a toy had outlived its usefulness?

I still keep my dachshund welcome mat by the front door.
It's my way of saying,
   "Please, come in," to all my canine friends.

CHAPTER 6

Closing Thoughts

We began this project by sharing our most indelible memories. It was quite a jumble at first, and we soon realized we needed to categorize, a task that became easier after hearing Lillian's poignant description of what she had experienced as a toddler in Paris. At our next meeting, we agreed that our opening chapter would be called "War Effects." A few months later we agreed on headings for our remaining chapters.

We knew that delving into the past might be painful, and sometimes it was. But it was also enlightening. As Anais Nin wrote in one of her essays, "We write to taste life twice, in the moment, and in retrospection." And so it was for us.

As we put these pages aside, we are reminded of how complex and frightening our world has become. It is our hope that the next and future generations take heed, and embrace the power of the written and spoken word to effect change. How different our lives might have been these past many years if Thomas Paine had not written *Common Sense*, if Abraham Lincoln had never delivered the *Gettysburg Address*, if Susan B. Anthony hadn't championed women's rights, if Rachel Carson hadn't given us *Silent Spring*.

Let us take our inspiration from them.

The Horrors of War

Lillian Lindy

War seems to be a constant thought I have had all my life. This is probably due to the fact that I was able to escape from Europe while the war was raging, and arrive in the United States in July 1941. My concern started in my teens when I met many people who had survived the war, or who had lost loved ones during that time, or had numbers on their arms from the camps.

In the 20th century alone, four major wars annihilated over **EIGHTY NINE MILLION** people. Note that this estimate is one of the lowest quoted, and that actual totals could be much higher. That is an incredible number, and it does not include lesser wars that occurred during that century. Apart from these horrible numbers, there is no way to calculate the effects on widows, orphans and children growing up without fathers. What about those casualties? What about those soldiers who never recover from their wounds either physically or mentally? What about people who are permanently displaced, those who face starvation? What about the cost of rebuilding lives, not to mention cities that have been destroyed?

So far, in the 21st century, there have not been any wars on the scale that we saw in the previous century. That does not mean that wars have ended. It only means that there are smaller wars everywhere on this earth with multitudes being killed, displaced, wounded or orphaned. The Syrian conflict alone has claimed over 580,000 lives. We live in a world where total annihilation is possible. China, France, Great Britain, India, Pakistan, Russia and the United States have nuclear weapons. Israel is widely believed to have them, and acquiring nuclear power is North Korea's number one goal. These facts alone are frightening.

The causes of war are one man with a lust for power, religious differences and/or economics or a combination of these factors. It would be hard to eliminate one person with that lust for power, but poor economic conditions give rise to that kind of despot.

To eliminate religious differences, governments need to teach tolerance.

To eliminate economic factors, we need to level the playing field so that countries suffering from poor economics, starvation etc., are provided with assistance for these problems. We live in one world, we are essentially one people. We must take care of those in need.

If we don't approach these problems with forceful action, regardless of what we do regarding climate change and other problems facing this earth, we will not solve the problem of war, and war will eliminate us.

The situation worries me greatly, but I pray that mankind will do the right thing.

The Past Lives On

Nancy Mather

I decided to write this memoir because I want my grandchildren to know more about my history. I want them to know that there is strength and will power in their genes, that they can overcome their difficulties and go on to have rewarding lives just as I have done.

I want them to know the past is always with us. I have recalled many people from the past whom I have loved. I have recalled others who have influenced me in some important way. There are also those who have disappointed me. I can look back to times fraught with the pain of loss or rich with the joy of discovery and say that I have learned from each of these experiences.

I have barely skimmed the surface of my many years. I have hardly touched on my parent's love for me and my sister. I have not written about my joy as a parent. Nor have I written about what it was like for my children to lose their father at a time when they most needed him.

I hope that what I have written will generate questions from my grandchildren for more information as well as give them a better understanding of who I am, this woman who happens to be their grandmother. I hope, too, that my friends and family will find this short memoir of interest, and agree that my life has been rich and rewarding. 🌸

Our Children Are Our Future

Bette Marafino

I have become increasingly concerned about the rapid acceleration of the negative effects of climate change and the inability of our current president and his followers to take this seriously, not only by denying scientific facts, but by passing legislation that will hasten climate change.

And so I was happy that my grandson Zachary, who is a junior in high school, joined the Coral Club at Hall High School. The club explores the importance of keeping our oceans healthy because so much of our lives is linked to this ecosystem. Their year-end activity was to host an Ocean Night. Eager students were on hand to talk about their environmental projects and the importance of saving our planet. An Australian documentary *Chasing Coral* was shown. This award winning documentary emphasized our dependence on healthy oceans and showed how rapidly warming waters are killing the coral reefs and sea life whose existence depends on a healthy ocean environment.

At this event, two middle school students had a table display which showed the damaging effects to ocean life of plastics discarded in the oceans. Their enthusiasm led them to attend a state legislative committee hearing to speak in favor of a bill that would limit single use plastic bags in the state. Their convincing arguments helped in the enactment of state legislation banning these plastic bags.

This is my concern. I worry that my children, grandchildren

and great-grandchildren will not have a healthy quality of life.
I applaud Zachary for his interest in helping to effect positive
change. So this is my message to my other grandchildren –
Aimee, Kristin, Elizabeth, James, Brian, Brendan, Michael,
Nicole and two great-grandsons – Andrew and Sam, work to
make changes for a healthier atmosphere for yourselves and
the generations to follow. 🌱

Making Sense of My World

Ketti Marks

It began when I was six or seven, the urge to write. I wrote, as little children do, about my child's world. When I was older and in college, I wrote poetry about the anguish and futility of war. I kept on writing after college. A multi-media script about the power of the sun. A mood piece about the sea. Last October, a readers theater script about the state of our nation.

Writing has been a part of me for a long time but it was only recently that I discovered my love of memoir. It is such a personal genre that I frequently find myself struggling to effect the proper balance between truth and creativity. Ultimately, my goal is to bring the reader into a piece of my world – to know some of the people I have known, to visit some of the places I have been, to be with me, if only for a moment or two. Above all else, to feel as I have felt.

When I registered for a memoir class in the fall of 2016 I had no idea how much I would like this new way of writing. I had rarely written dialogue before, and it was a challenge to familiarize myself with the basics. I hadn't paid much attention to voice, and that was a challenge, too. I found myself welcoming these challenges. But most of all, memoir reinforced my belief that the right word, the right detail, even the right sentence fragment—can determine how a reader responds to a story. I still have a lot to learn about memoir, and I am looking forward to it.

Biography

Lillian Lindy

I was born in Paris, France and immigrated to the United States when I was five years old. My family settled in New York City.

My parents believed in education, religious upbringing, and learning about music, dance and the arts. I went to private schools and took piano and dance lessons as well as religious classes. They also believed in a strict upbringing, not onerous but strict. I would never go against their wishes.

New York City was a great place to grow up in with all that it had to offer. On Saturdays I would go to the Museum of Natural History where they had a huge dinosaur and an exhibit of human embryos at various stages of growth. Other times I would go to the movies where double features, along with a newsreel and a cartoon, were shown. We used to bring our lunch and spend the entire afternoon at the movie house.

I lived near Central Park. That park was my playground.

I roller-skated, biked and rode horses in this beautiful space. The city was a very safe place at that time. We could play in the streets without any concern. Stoop ball was one of my favorite games.

When I was eleven, my mother died, and within a few years everything changed. My father remarried a wonderful woman, and I moved to France where I stayed for almost two years. My stay there was terrific, and I returned to go to college.

Then life brought me to Connecticut and here I remain in a place I really enjoy.

As with others, I have had wonderful times and terrible times in my life, but the good always outweighed the bad. All in all, life has been good to me. 🌱

Nancy Mather

I was born in Brooklyn, New York in May 1930 to Italian parents who had emigrated from Italy to the United States in 1921. They disembarked at Ellis Island within months of each other, and met four years later. They married in 1928. My sister and only sibling came along in 1932.

We were a close-knit family. My father was a typical Sicilian father. He was strict, demanding, and overly protective. Yet he was loving. He made sure I was exposed to the beauties of the natural world - to music, to art, to literature. My mother was loving, too. Her world centered on her daughters. When coming home from school I would often find her sitting in the enclosed sun porch, needle in hand, embroidering a flower or leaf on a cloth tightly stretched through the rings of a hoop, the embroidered item to be saved for a trousseau. In the kitchen, one of her delicious soups or pasta sauces would be simmering away. She was an inventive and intuitive cook, and we often said that she sprinkled magic, along with salt, on her food.

Our neighbors were German, Irish, Italian, and Jewish. Their children were my neighborhood friends. We played hopscotch on a chalk grid we drew on the sidewalk. We jumped rope and skated together on streets that were practically empty of cars.

We had a movie house around the corner and we often went to the Saturday morning matinees. My father always made sure my sister and I had enough money for the cost of admission plus a candy bar.

How lucky I am to have grown up where I did! To me, even though I've lived in Connecticut for many years, Brooklyn is the true center of the Universe. ❧

Bette Marafino

I grew up in an Irish-Polish family in New Britain,
Connecticut. I was the oldest of three sisters. We attended
public schools and did the things that families usually do.
From the second grade, I knew I wanted to be a teacher and
I had the good fortune to live within walking distance of
Teachers College of Connecticut. I say good fortune because
there was no way my family could afford to send me away to
college.

I met my husband in college and we married the summer
of our graduation. We've spent many years teaching in
both the public schools and in the Connecticut Community
College system. Raising a family and involvement in the
union movement was also a part of our very active life. Our
family continues to grow with four married adult children,
nine grandchildren, and two infant great-grandsons.

Because I grew up in a union household, my inclination

toward the union movement led me to assume leadership roles in the Congress of Connecticut Community Colleges union (4Cs), including a six-year term as its president. Now that I'm retired, I continue to stay active in social justice issues. I serve as president of the Connecticut Alliance for Retired Americans (ARA) which is a part of the AFL/CIO. 🌱

Ketti Marks

I was born into a family of non-conformists. Growing up, my father introduced me to writers and activists like Lincoln Steffens, Eugene V. Debs, and Upton Sinclair. My mother told me stories about how she bucked the system in nursing school when it was the right thing to do. As for myself, I was a bit too young to participate in the early years of the civil rights movement but my sister kept up the family tradition by going to Maryland to protest Jim Crow.

Like many teenagers living in New York City in the nineteen sixties, I attended City University. I graduated from Hunter College with a B.A. in Speech and Theater and later earned an M.A. in Rhetoric and Public Address from Brooklyn College.

While going for my Master's, I worked part-time editing and speech-writing for the Earl G. Graves publishing company, and also taught introductory speech courses at

Brooklyn College.

In the early '80s I began teaching English and coaching debate at Midwood High School in Brooklyn, New York. More recently, I have been taking classes, including memoir writing, at the University of Hartford. After the 2016 election I joined TALK, an organization formed in Glastonbury to promote civil dialogue and active citizen participation in government. I have also spoken at community groups in Connecticut on the significance and structure of Lincoln-Douglas debate as well as on George Orwell's *1984* and its relevancy today.

The End

Bette Marafino
982 N Main St
W H 06117-2054

Made in the USA
Columbia, SC
12 July 2020

13001305R00088